poems
for
Grenfell
Tower

The Onslaught Press

Published by The Onslaught Press
30 March 2018

1. Poems © 2018 **The poets listed on the contents page**

2. Foreword © 2018 **David Lammy, MP**

3. Cover photograph © 2018 & courtesy of **Emily Clack Moulden**

4. Cover design & this edition © 2018 **Mathew Staunton**

ISBN: **978-1-912111-55-8**

The front cover is set in Habel by Creativertacos; the poems and titles in Le Monde Livre, Kefa and Nanum Myeongjo; and the back cover texts in Le Monde Sans. The dedications page opposite was typeset by Michael Everson in Gentium Plus, Babelstone Han, Bangla MT, Devanagari MT, DT Naskh, DT Nastaliq, DT Nastaliq Press, Gujarati MT, Gurmukhi MT, Kefa, Nanum Myeongjo, Sinhala MT, Tamil MT, and Toppan Bunkyu Mincho. Many thanks to him for that.

Printed & bound by Lightning Source

Ɛnkɔ mma wɔn a Grenfell abrosan atɔrenkyɛm no kaa wɔn no

ለጉጓዱ◌ ህጓ9 ቃጠሱ 7ዳ+ቅፑ

من اجل ضحايا حريق برج غرينفيل

গ্রেনফেল টাওয়ার অগ্নিকাণ্ডের ক্ষতিগ্রস্তদের জন্য

Den Opfern des Brandes im Grenfell Tower

Για τα θύματα της πυρκαγιάς του Πύργου του Γκρένφελ

For the victims of the Grenfell Tower fire

Para las víctimas del incendio de la Torre de Grenfell

برای قربانیان آتش سوزی برج کرنفل

Pour les victimes de l'incendie de la tour Grenfell

Ke ha maa ni gbo ye Grenfell

ગ્રેનફેલ ટાવરની આગ ના ભોગ બનેલા લોકો માટ

עבור קורבנות השר פה במגדל גרנפ

ग्रेनफेल टावर के पीड़ितों के लिए

Pou sé moun-la ki pèd lavi-yó an difé Grenfèl

Màkà ndi nwúrú n'ọkụ gbárá nà Tọ́wà Grénfèl.

Per le vittime dell'incendio della Torre di Grenfell

グレンフェル・タワー火災の犠牲者のために

Fi aal uu ded ina di Grenfel Touwa faiya

그렌펠 타워 화재의 피해자를 위하여

Ji bo qurbaniyên Grenfell Tower agir

A bakosebwa mu Grenfell Tower

Mpɔ na baviktím ya mŏtɔ epelákí na Grenfell Tower

ਗ੍ਰੇਨਫੈਲ ਟਾਵਰ ਅੱਗ ਦੇ ਸ਼ਿਕਾਰ ਲੋਕਾਂ ਲਈ

Dla ofiar pożaru w Grenfell Tower

دکرینفیل برج وقربانیا نولپاره

Para as vítimas do incêndio da Torre Grenfell

Жертвам пожара в башне Гренфелл-Тауэр

ഗ്രെത്തെൾ ‍ടവരയേ ‍ഗീത്തെത് ‍ടിഥാ ‍വിദ്ത്തത് സഛഥാ

Waxaa loogu talo galay dhibbanayaasha Grenfell Tower dab

Për viktimat e zjarrit të kullës Grenfell

За настрадале у пожару у Гренфел Тауера

Kwa waathirika wa moto wa Grenfell Tower

கிரென்ஃபெல் கட்டடத் தீ விபத்தில் பாதிக்கப்பட்டவர்களுக்காக

ስለ ሕነ1 7ሪ1ሯ⌂ ዝ+∧8∧ በርበ ሐዋ 1ዞ+7ዄኮ

Para sa mga biktima ng sunog ng Grenfell Tower

Grenfell Kulesi yangını kurbanları anısına

گرینفیسل ٹاورآ آتش زدگے کے متاثرین کے نام

Cho các nạn nhân của ngọn lửa Tòa nhà Grenfell

Fun awọn olufaragba Ibon Grenfell Tower

給予格倫費塔大火的受害者

Foreword

Grenfell Tower exposed a tale of two cities: one that has a voice, and one that does not.

Situated in the wealthy borough of Kensington and Chelsea, Grenfell was home to those whose voices were unheard by people in power. Residents found themselves repeatedly ignored by the authorities—their concerns about the safety of Grenfell were brushed off, and their worries fell on deaf ears. Instead of listening to them, the council neglected their warnings and retreated into the shadows.

Tragically, we have seen how after the disaster, as Grenfell leaves the headlines and media attention wanes, the residents of Grenfell are still not being heard. Seven months on, many don't have a permanent home, and are being forced to live in a state of uncertainty. The government's promises have proved to be empty, and it feels increasingly as if they are once again being forgotten. As Ben Okri poignantly expressed on Channel 4 at the time, in his poem 'Grenfell Tower, June 2017', in Grenfell we saw how '*a sword of fate hangs over the deafness of power*'. Yet, the powerful continue to be deaf to Grenfell's voices and voices of those like them.

Poems for Grenfell Tower encourages readers to listen and bear witness to the human cost of Grenfell. The poems are able to express the scale of loss, in a way that prose is not able to do—from the empty school chair invoked in Michael Rosen's piece, to Rachel Burns's 'In a Hotel Room, A Father Sits Alone'. Unlike countless newspaper articles and reports in the media, poetry goes some of the way in allowing the reader to understand what is really missing—a child in a schoolroom, a much loved daughter.

Poems for Grenfell Tower brings together many different poets, whose voices are joined together in elegy. Ricky Nuttall, a Red Watch firefighter who attended Grenfell, offers a heart-wrenching account of coming to terms with what happened. His heroism is reinforced by Christine Barton's 'Red Watch', which pays a moving tribute to the work of firefighters. Poems such as these are able to go beyond the limits of prose in expressing the impact of the tragedy. In doing so, they offer an important way in which the voices of Grenfell are heard.

The Right Honourable David Lammy, MP

Thanks

I am very grateful to everyone who put this book together or is now helping to promote it, including:

Mathew Staunton at The Onslaught Press, for friendship, support, and tireless care for every aspect of the book; David Lammy, MP, for his clear and trenchant Foreword; the members of the selection panel, who prefer not to be named, for assessing and choosing from about 350 poems; FaceBook friends and contributors to the book, who obtained the translations for the Dedication; Michael Everson, the linguistics expert who oversaw the typography of the Dedication; Emily Clack Moulden, of White City, for the photograph on the front cover; the members of the public who provided endorsements for our back cover; the management and staff of the Harrow Social Club, North Kensington, and of the Seven Dials Club in Covent Garden, for hosting our launches without charge; Robb Johnson, Nostalgia Steelband, Rihab Azar, and RAKA, for playing at the launches; the organizers of related events planned for several places across Britain in the coming months; more than 330 poets from Britain and across the world who offered their poems, solidarity, and support; the 62 poets who appear here, for tolerating my various proposals and delivering what was asked of them; and lastly but especially those amongst them who bore my thoughts and queries about their cherished work with good heart and open minds, with the single shared aim of presenting good poetry in support of justice and social change.

It was a sad privilege to create this book.

The editor

A note to the reader

Most of the poems are direct responses to the burning of Grenfell Tower on 14 June 2017, a sight which, in the words of Sadiq Khan, Mayor of London, 'should be forever seared into our nation's collective memory'. A few were written in other circumstances, but have been included because they deal with factors in British society which may have contributed to the Grenfell disaster, or with aspects of such disasters in general.

An asterisk below an author's name shows that their poem has an entry in the Notes and Acknowledgements section. Four poems not in English have translations beside them.

Lastly, at the suggestion of Grenfell United, all royalties will go to the Grenfell Foundation. The amount raised will be reported on the book's FaceBook page.

Grenfell, 2018

So, pull down the monument of Britain's shame?
It's not enough. The horror and the grief
May some day ease; insomnia and strain
Give ground before the impetus of life.
And perhaps the dead have other things in mind
Than Grenfell Night, more practical concerns . . .
But years will not dispel the stench of crime.
The cremated steel and concrete ghost will scorn
Mere demolition; rather, persevere
For children's children's schoolchildren to read
And wonder, with stilled hands and hidden care,
At how their ancestors were torched for greed,
But then the neighbourhood rose up through fire
To stand together, one with Grenfell Tower.

The editor
March 2018
*

Souad's Moon

You explain how your family lives two seas away.
Mountains rise between you, guards patrol their streets.

Hope is a fierce dove that risks everything to stay alive
and you have done with messages of fire.

You've travelled far to escape a lifetime of running.
You cannot be there and they cannot be here.

But there is always your dream: one day they will
find themselves unaccountably weightless and free

and you, equally beyond Earth's tether,
will meet them, widowed sisters and aunts,

and hold their dear remembered faces
between your hands again.

Pat Winslow
Hailey, Oxfordshire

High-Rise

Apply online. Get shortlisted. Buy a suit. Bullshit your
way through the interview using non-sequitur
as a route to saying nothing to contradict the fake CV.
Bingo. Buy a car. Bye bye buses. Buy into the lie
that the Arms-length Management Organization
you are now local manager for is not a job creation
scheme for cowboy builders. Take your first bribe.
Buy a bigger car. Wear hi-viz. Pretend to drive a JCB
for the photo op with the Housing Minister. Smile.
Buy a dental plan. Private healthcare. To reconcile
your conscience, buy a seat on the council. Your vote
counts. Helping local communities prosper. End quote.
Buy a flat in a tower block. Rent it out. It's on a higher
floor. That view. Those sundowns set the place on fire.

Al McClimens
Sheffield
*

Border Patrol

First they made me empty my heart. My parents laid out side by side.
Papa still in his stupid hat, mama in the dress she wore at the last
wedding we all went to.

Next they made me empty my conscience. One brother, younger, left
behind. I knew they'd be coming and I didn't go back to warn him.
I hid in the shadows, and took my chance to escape when they'd gone.

Then they made me empty my memories. Anna at the architect's
party where she got so drunk we had to stop the taxi on the way
home so she could throw up by the side of the road.

Lastly they asked me to empty my faith. A house with a small garden
where you can sit in the evenings and listen to the trains. Neighbours
you aren't afraid of.

Finally they said I was free to go. I thought of leaving it all behind,
but I'm like a man whose suit is stretched out of shape by all the
things he keeps in his pockets.

He complains, but he cannot bear to buy a new one.

Matt Barnard
Brent
*

The Bunker

Our seedy tower block sits on top of a Cold War nuclear bunker,
both of them the work of cowboy builders
who died in mysterious circumstances in the 1970s.
Even now, after years of demanding answers,
no one is prepared to address our concerns,
which concern a structure that, officially, doesn't exist.

I wasn't alive in 1965 when the Ministry of Secret Buildings,
continuing to keep the bunker's location secret,
failed to inform the Ministry of Misconceived Ideas,
which allowed our high-rise flats to be built on top.

I was very much alive though in 1991 when I inadvertently
discovered the bunker's entrance late one evening.
Hearing cries for help in dense shrubs near our block,
I found a loose man-hole cover and, descending a rusty ladder
into a huge sprawling concrete complex,
was shocked to stumble upon charred human remains.
Terrified, I ran straight out and rang the police,
but after bundling me into their car the plain clothes
slipped acid into my tea at the station
and charged me with possession and making a false report
while under the influence. By the time the charges were dropped,
the cash-strapped council had hurriedly built a basketball court
at the very spot where the entrance had been.

Well, here I am, still just about alive in 2017.
Hard experience has made me realize what we're up against,
but the bunker—a ticking time bomb—remains beneath us,
and although that acid trip might have clouded my memory,
and maybe the bunker never was filled up with burnt bodies,
it still needs to be condemned, along with our block—

two Cold War relics that have no place in the 21st century.
And it's not just me: most residents too have come to realize
that the government's trying to hide an omen.
Let's face it: every time they claim there's nothing there,
but won't explain why info concerning that space is 'classified',
they are simply making it obvious the bunker does exist
and I wasn't off my head. Meanwhile, fearing a cover-up,
residents worry that this shoddily-built structure we inhabit—
undermined by the crumbling bunker—will eventually collapse.

But I know what I saw and, even if it was all just in my mind,
it portends a fate that's even worse—
that what the bunker never had to be used for
may someday be unleashed after all, like a stored-up curse,
as destructive as a nuclear blast, but more concentrated,
swirling up as a circling furious fire, then collapsing catastrophically
into black holes that once were windows.

Tom McColl
Newham
*

A Report from the Border

Wars in peacetime don't behave like wars.
So loving they are.
Kissed on both cheeks, silk-lined ambassadors
Pose and confer.

> *Unbuckle your envy, drop it there by the door.*
> *We will settle,*
> *We will settle without blows or bullets*
> *The unequal score.*

> *In nature, havenots have to be many*
> *And havelots few.*
> *Making money out of making money*
> *Helps us help you.*

This from the party of good intent. From the other,
Hunger's stare,
Drowned crops, charred hopes, fear, stupor, prayer,
And literature.

Anne Stevenson
Durham
*

Wrong Move

found on home rental agency website

Fabulous bright 2 bedroom flat
3 minutes walk to Latimer Road tube station,
18th floor of newly renovated Grenfell Tower,
panoramic views of London landmarks,
77 square metres in size.

What is there not to like?

Contemporary fully fitted kitchen,
open plan living room,
2 double bedrooms with fitted wardrobes,
limestone bathroom, office area
along open space in hallway,
ample storage space.

It could have been me.

Well insulated,
close to all the amenities:
walking distance from Ladbroke Grove and Portobello Market,
easy reach from Westfields shopping centre,
inclusive of council tax.

You could see your life there so easily.

Gym/sport centre nearby,
excellent restaurants,
trendy buzzing social scene.
Available to move in from 17 October 2016.
Minimum tenancy term is 12 months.

And the half is not told.
I cannot count how much it cost.

Jane Spiro
Eynsham, Oxfordshire

*

Post Mortem

It was a disaster, of course.
Many people died before it ended.
No one knew how many exactly
because counting the bodies was so hard.
The figures were fudged anyway
so people say.
Some lucky ones escaped.
There were witnesses.
As to the cause of it
even now it's hard to be sure.
Most likely it started in a dry goods store
just around the corner from the Circus.
It was windy that night
and the fire spread in gusts.
So many people so much dry wood.
Some of the apartments
those nearest centre
were razed to the ground within minutes.
Others on the edges
remained standing for weeks
charred and empty ghosts
of what they were.
Then officials came down
wearing solemn expressions
and poked about the ashes for hours
while the Emperor, Jove bless him,
opened his garden for the homeless
and the poor to pitch their tents.
Still there were rumours.

It was said by some that the looters
were in the pay of Nero.
Others claimed to have heard it
from those who knew
how the Emperor came running
hotfoot from Antium
to rescue his many works of art.
All we know for certain
is that when it came down to it
they blamed the whole business
on the Christians.
There were public executions
a bit of a spectacle
then Nero rebuilt
in grand style.

Abigail Elizabeth Rowland
Penzance

Partitions, 1982

'... among the multitudes
Of that great City, oftentimes was seen
Affectingly set forth, more than elsewhere
Is possible, the unity of man,
One spirit over ignorance and vice
Predominant, in good and evil hearts;
One sense for moral judgments, as one eye
For the sun's light.'

My nose angles the air,
a little missile edged into the sunset,
little receiver, the indigenous one
who doesn't belong,
sensing an odour of fascism
round a lack of generosity
like the swelling round an inoculation
gone wrong.

Newspapermen prowl the dusk
attacking strangers,
ribbing out their flesh
which hangs in colours on the line
to warn of habitation and strict ways.
In the ensuing dark, queues form
for doctors.

But this old basement laundry fought for,
the washing-slabs gone
with grandmother's solid arms;

then control of it,
a community centre
bandaged with posters,
playgroups fought for,
and why not, for every child,
a possibility and an open door?

Steve Griffiths
Ludlow
*

Work-Around

Had such a day at work, running around:
the meetings, the changes to keep the costs down.
And they've had second thoughts about colours again,
the clients are stupid, it's really insane —
first it was 'silver zinc', now it's 'champagne'.
But I've sourced the new colour, saved 300K,
downgraded the windows and found cheaper frames,
the landscaping's scrapped — it would just go to waste,
so now we're on budget, or nearly at least.
And today I've achieved what's expected of me:
keep management happy, keep customers sweet,
keep projects on track — bloody hell, quite a feat.
But they take you for granted, it's always the same,
I call that a scandal, I call it a shame.

Meg Barton
Oxford

due diligence

let's finesse a death trap
in the sky, why don't we
let's forget almost
it's there, till we stare
at the desperate
wavers of makeshift flags
flaming   flaming   flaming
the polyglot people
of Lancaster West
screaming   screaming   screaming
till they shock
with their silence

Sam Phipps
Edinburgh

The Burning of the House

The burning of the house was the last thing.
The blackened faces, limbs, and the charred ground
covered in ash, the smoke to make eyes sting.

It runs a harsh truth down to the last pound.
The pavement burns with sun. The walls are hot.
The wound is raw: we leave things as they're found.

We find them so, attend to them or not,
And go about our business till it's raw.
There is no narrative, no scheme or plot,

It's just the system, just another flaw.
They burn and burn. Things go up in a flash.
It is the debris that sticks in the craw,

The burnt-down matchsticks, ashtrays full of ash,
The windings of the process, profit, loss,
The broken sky, the smoke, the weightless cash

That burns right down but rises from the dross.
Our throats are parched, it's getting hard to breathe,
Though in the street the branches lightly toss.

George Szirtes
Wymondham, Norfolk

Red Watch

'We've never worked harder. We gave everything.
Sorry it wasn't enough. R.I.P. Love, Red Watch Firefighters'

We used to look forward to your coming—
Fit young men and feisty young women in uniforms
Guaranteed to raise a smile.

Pictures for the newsletter of kids grinning widely
Wearing your over-sized gear
Sitting in the cab pressing buttons
Giggling as the siren reverberated under the motorway,
Making the teachers jump in mock alarm.

You'd squat down, on their level,
Encouraging the nervous ones to take a turn with the hose
Restraining those cheeky ones
Who had their own ideas about where to direct it.
Laughter.

Then out in the garden
Down the pole on the climbing frame;
Who wants a go? Me! Me! Me!

Cheap plastic helmets from the dressing up box
Ladder up against the playhouse
Dolls rescued from the cardboard flames

Stickers all round
Leaflets for your mums and dads
Keep safe kids

Did our little ones remember you that night,
Waiting for the rescue that could not come?

We know that you remembered them.
We know that you fought for them,
Up those smoke-filled stairwells.
We know you would have died for them.

So know that we remember you
With love
Our Red Watch heroes.

Christine Barton
Bath

Field of Crimson

On Sunday 2nd September 1666
a bakery in Pudding Lane, a stone's throw from the River Thames,
sparks fire among the City's rancid streets,

where masses of labourers, tradesmen, paupers,
grudgingly given space beside the rich,
live and work inside a teeming maze.

Lord Mayor Thomas Bloodworth,
woken to be informed, replies 'Pish! A woman might piss it out'.
But the flames' spite spreads.

Among families and workers,
bemusement turns to concern, fear to horror and disbelief,
as row after row of homes, stores and workshops

fall prey to a monster far vaster and equally as malevolent
as Beowulf's night-wraith foe Grendel;
even for the bravest, no way in to this field of furious crimson;

for those bewildered, hobbled, fevered,
there's no way out. Volunteers grip at a scattering of buckets,
carts with water tanks arrive too late with pipes of limited reach.

Tears smear smoke-darkened faces.
Hard to say which is worse—the human cries, or aftermath.
Ash of bone leaves no obvious trace for those that tally the dead.

In the weeks to come, some advisers to the King
try hard to forget hints they'd received of inferno risks.
Others look upon levelled smouldering black

and squabble over architects, engineers, and scapegoats.
Five months on, a plan to rebuild is worked out, with assent
granted by Charles II. At which a few wonder if,

the changes forced, to construct in safe brick and stone
and manageable height, promise some good from disaster—
for the sake of sanity, change that must not be undone.

Neil Reeder
Westminster

*

And in the Air Death Moans and Sings

It was scribbled down the sides of the buildings in Manhattan.
It flashes out of a chamber of the Great Pyramid's heart.
It is waving at a taffrail, hangs over that open hatch
or from a high forbidden ledge on a peak still unrecorded.

And if you can read it, one of all those hundred tongues,
but the one the inhabitants of Last Resort know best,
you will know what it means. Not *escape*, no, that is
a false friend, who'll get you nowhere: the true translation

is *help us, help us, please*. But theirs is a dead language,
and there are too many coins, heads up, blocking
the access road with crowns, and too many eyes are closed
ready for them. Into the flames go the fat-rich notes

like leaves from a money-tree, whose roots were never removed:
it flowers yellow, it fruits red. Here, they set
new forests for the world's forgotten people to hide in,
where now the final signal falls from that high comradeship.

John Greening
St Neots, Cambridgeshire
*

The Firefighter

I'm staring blankly
Frankly I'm broken
My heart can't be mended
Befriended or woken

An emptiness consumes me
In sorrow I'm soaked
My words can't be heard
As I'm strangled and choked

As tears stripe each cheek
With a trail of sadness
My soul is stained black
With the screams With the madness

The pain of such tragedy
The waste of such life
The death of a husband
His children   His wife

The stairs were too many
My breaths were too few
My body exhausted
Now mentally too

The silence of death
My smoke-stained hair
A hole in my soul
That will never repair

The feeling of failure
And pride that combine
To leave me confused
And abused in my mind

My lips wet with tears
I am lost   There's no plan
Emotionally ruined
One broken man

Ricky Nuttall
Red Watch, Battersea Fire Station

In a Hotel Room, a Father sits Alone

In a hotel room, a father sits alone
thinks about his little girl
her voice on the phone
he sees the mighty flames unfurl.

He thinks about his little girl
the neighbour's cries, as smoke billows
he sees the mighty flames unfurl,
the faces pressed to high windows.

The neighbour's cries, as smoke billows
trapped in Grenfell's burning tower
faces pressed to high windows.
Help in bold, pressed to glass, the final hour.

They are trapped in Grenfell's burning tower.
Still screaming. We hear them dying.
Help in bold, pressed to glass, the final hour.
Her daddy's eyes red from crying.

They are still screaming. We hear them dying.
We are powerless to do anything.
Her daddy's eyes red from crying.
He has lost everything.

We are powerless to do anything.
We watch them jump to their death.
He has lost everything.
He hears his daughter's last gasp for breath.

We watch them jump to their death
the flames licking the high-rise glass.
He hears his daughter's last gasp for breath.
People talk about social class.

The flames are licking the high-rise glass
a furnace rises up through the floors.
People talk about social class.
People talk about housing policy, class wars.

A furnace rises up through the floors.
She tells her father there is so much smoke.
People talk about housing policy, class wars.
He listens as she chokes, as she chokes.

She tells her father there is so much smoke.
He hears her voice on the phone.
Listens to her as she chokes, as she chokes.
In a hotel room, a father sits alone.

Rachel Burns
Durham

The Death of Children

It is the death of children most offends
nature and justice. No use asking why.
What justice is, nobody comprehends.

What punishment can ever make amends?
There's no pretext, excuse or alibi.
It is the death of children most offends.

Whoever offers arguments pretends
to read fate's lines. Although we must swear by
what justice is, nobody comprehends

how destiny or chance weaves. Who defends
their motives with fair reasons tells a lie.
It is the death of children most offends.

Death can't deserve to reap such dividends
from these, who scarcely lived, their parents cry.
What justice is, nobody comprehends.

Bring comfort then, and courage. Strangers, friends,
are we not all parents when children die?
What justice is, nobody comprehends.
It is the death of children most offends.

Richard Berengarten
Cambridge
*

Sara

Backed across the ocean
of that small room, a woman in a black dress
who always knew which foot to put first.
There is nothing
living, which isn't on a journey.

That dress, fine
part of yourself, skin, flesh, two hundred and six bones.
Bismillahi, sister —
obey the frightened animals of your eyes
and leave this corner.

Julie Lumsden
Chesterfield

Storytime

Mama, what is that sound?
Is it the leaves in the trees
that rustle and shake and
make us awake?

Mama, must we stay? Is it right
that the night becomes light?
Have you made me a cake
with candles that flicker
so bright?

Why are you cold, Mama?
It is hot like a day when
we go to the park, and I play
on the swings swooping
higher and higher.

Why are you crying, Mama?
Tell me the story you keep
in your head. The one with
the lion that comes to the door,
with a roar, and asks to be fed.

And you make him a sandwich
with honey and bread
and he climbs on the bed
and you say it's the night

when we sleep that makes
everything right. Tomorrow
poor lion you can come out to play.
What will the neighbours say?

Mama don't be afraid. Do you
want us to pray? I know what
to say. We're both in a rocket
and we're going away. That's
the sound

           that we hear,
and that's why it's bright with
a dancing light. And we'll soar
into space to a beautiful place
where everyone's kind and
they care for each other and

you'll never again be
frightened and cold and I'll
live to be a hundred years old.
Mama! Hold me tight.

Andrew Dixon
Oxford

Hanako Paints Hiroshima

Afterwards, grown-ups whisper
stories of survival, minor miracles.
How Mr Tanaka was shielded
from the blast by concrete pillars
in his storeroom; how some slaked
their thirst on black rain; how the temple
ginkgo had endured with just a scorch.
This gave them hope.

She sits with her pastels. Bold strokes
create the Ota river, flowing clear,
to cool the scalding earth beneath her feet
as she escapes encroaching fire. She presses
hard on shades of green, outlines the Chugoku
hills around the city, blots out spectres
of smoke and ash. And in the distance,
inky birds sketched against an August sky,
wings outstretched like screaming arms.

Margaret Beston
Tonbridge
*

The Day After

Her back is bent.
She spent the night
searching the flames.

Eyes, red-rimmed,
not from smoke alone,
never sway from the scene.

A friendly hand reaches out
to shoulder the pain.
Words pierce her ears,

Don't give up hope—
pass through, leave no trace
beyond a shudder.

No, she shakes her head.
She's an obedient child—
when told to stay, she stays.

Sharon Cohagan
Bonn

this grief is partisan

even the air sighs for us
this grief is one breath
this grief is the hum of nine poets
this grief has peeled skin
it is not shielded
from

lies, evasions
dissuasions

this grief
is a procession
this grief is an army of tears
the sun will not scorch it
the rain cannot drown it

this empty room
this charred field
this quiet road in the kernel of night
this aching of many hearts
this gallery of loss

our grief weaves a ribbon for flowers
oh small flower
oh white petal
even the birds cry for us
even the moon keeps silent

S.O. Fasrus
Islington
*

36

Carnival

Enjoy but

samba slower

passing the Tower

Briefly remember when
softly beating samba drum
not the crematorium become
but the wretchedness of this destroying
the lost and damaged, all deserving more

Black box skeleton looms
(no more photos please today)
charcoal-sketched into multi-grey
darkly-etched against the blue of summer
contrasting with your brightness and colour

When a festival
becomes a tribute
on an out-of-season
dia de los muertos

just samba slower

past the Tower

samba slower

Peter A. Kelly
Airdrie, North Lanarkshire
*

In this Space We do Not Breathe

for Khadija Saye

My dreams are troubled

as if a fire had roared a silver river
ash trembled into negative
through a doorless arch

as if an eye had lost its lid
a camera its shutter
left open to outstare the sky

as if brick had fused with pain
become tethered
become votive

no one will now explain
how her later works
eclipsed her early prints

no one will speculate
whether genius was unflinching
if she faltered in her forties
or flowered late

my dreams are troubled
by the current's roiling spate
as if history is still drowning

and somewhere above me
a fire is still a silver river

Gillian Laker
Canterbury
*

38

How do you Rehearse for This?

Someone switches the warehouse radio off,
a signal for another one minute vigil
and the noisy office falls silent like an audience
sensing a show's about to begin.
The ash and black tower block skeleton
could belong to a flickering war movie.
Critics shout who the murderer is before
a blaze of detectives secure the scene,
even before the victims are known.
In the interval the audience donate
to crowdfunders, and open homes.
The director hides in the bar, the prompter
loses the script, the technician can't manoeuvre
the spotlight. There's a call for the scriptwriter,
who's suffering from concussion after walking
into a lighting rig the floor manager failed
to move, and clings desperately to anything
but the truth. The lights splutter out.
The stage turns cold and looks even darker.
The players are abandoned.
Survivors blink at their new-found fame
but fifteen minutes now is worse than the prior
waiting in the wings, shushed into accepting
cut corners, poor wiring and cheap costumery.
The audience take their selfies and move on.
The players sense they are supposed to shuffle
off stage. They put one foot forward, testing
their weight on the boards, fingers outstretched
to feel for obstacles as they inch towards shadows.

Emma Lee
Leicester

Grenfell, where Souls Billow

Your skin was the silken wrapping of an exquisite gift;
it was not you.

Your bones were the sculpted struts of an elegant frame;
they were not you.

Your blood was the ebb and flow which washed the dark shores;
it was not you.

Your fingerprints were maps of where you had been, and would go;
they were not you.

The dust that remains chokes me,
but it is not you.

You were deep inside all that,
and panoramic outside all that.
You were and are
a weightless energy that fills my space,
a close-grained essence of you.
I am awash, brimful
of your thick and palpable spirit,
your unfiltered memory.

Your soul is no feather, wafted on a breeze.
I am swathed in it,
heavy with it.
The flames devoured your flesh, but they set your spirit free —

and that is the part that is you.

Helen Laycock
Chalfont St Peter, Buckinghamshire

Painted Ladies

They came from Africa; in waves.
On wings of gold, filled with grit
and fragility, those butterflies flew.
flashes of flame with black-spot tips
They fled, stained-glass survivors,
to Kensington; met the hummingbird
hawk-moth, on respite from Spain
migrants in search of relief from heat
and settled. They shared the space
with an engineer, an artist swathed
in fabrics of joy, with mothers, sons
eyes ablaze with fervour and life
from Syria, lovers from Italy, poets,
Columbian daughters, architects,
philosophers, Filipinos, Logan-to-be.
drawn by fate to a toxic pyre
Songs of the Mediterranean blue rock
thrush mingled with Urdu and Farsi,
with flavours of salt fish and cumin.
till the night of sirens, fumes and prayers
when remnants of gossamer hindwings
and red mosaic capes fluttered to earth
with unfinished homework and ash.

Bernadette Lynch
Birmingham

Selfie

Watch me.

Through the crowd I stand tall
though my spine
has been crumpled, folded and unfolded
by fumbling, lazy fingers,
my skin may be peeling
and shedding
but people still call me
home
these people sleep between my ribs
tuck dreams under tissue
and tired responsibilities
right next to my heart.

Watch.

Every beat is the crack
of concrete under cautious feet
or the rattling of walls
from loud mouths
and music and meaning
every beat pumps stories
through otherwise hollow veins
these arteries are clogged with secrets—
it's all tinder.

And when you insulate lungs
with lies and loose change
I am bound to go up
in flames.

Watch me burn,

disintegrate, as dust
covers up the last reminders.
These broken bones are gravestones.

I keep epitaphs under my tongue
because one day someone
will be allowed to listen.

Chelsea Stockham
Bristol

The Voices of Grenfell Tower

Hashim calling   calling
Hashim's wife calling calling
Hashim's three children calling   calling
look! the fire consumed a building
now it is consuming me
with all the burning voices of the dead
old people   young people
      Marco calling   calling
boys and girls everyone I used to see
      Zainab calling   calling
and say hello to at the bus stop
      Bernard calling   calling
or the train station on Latimer Road
      Nura calling   calling
voices wailing into their twisted mobiles
      Hania and Esra calling   calling
about the stairs and the smoke
even if they have no eyes to see the building
or live in it now without their bodies
      Anthony calling   calling
even if their kind words and smiles in the street
      Mariem calling   calling
have all gone up in smoke
      Jeremiah calling   calling
we shared this ground
now I bear witness to their disappearance
oh! burning souls have burning voices
let me be their guarantee of truth!

የግሪንፊል ህንፃ ድምፆች

ሃሺምም ይጣራል! ይጣራል! ይጣራል!
የባለቤቱም ድምጿ፣ ይጣራል! ይጣራል!
የሶስት ልጆቹም ድምፆ፣ ይጣራል! ይጣራል!
ህንፃ ጔሪ አቃጥሎ፣ ያ ጨካኝ ነበልባል፣
አሁንም ባሳቤ፣ ሁልዬ ይነዷል፣
አዋ እሰማለሁኝ፣ የሚነዱ ድምፆች፣ ከተቃጠሉት፣
ከአዳጊ ወጣቶች፣ ባልቴት፣ አዛውንት፣
      አዋ! ማርኮም አለ! ይጣራል! ይጣራል!
የወንዶች፣ የሴቶች፣ የማወቃቸው ሁሉ ድምፃቸው ይሰማል፣
      አዋ! የዘይነባም! ይጣራል! ይጣራል!
ካውቶቡስ ማቆሚያው፣ ሰላም ጎረቤቴ፣ እንደት አደርክ ይላል፣
      በርናርድም ይጣራል! ይጣራል! ይጣራል!
ላቲመር መንገድ ላይ፣ አባቡሩ ጣቢያ፣ ብዙ ተያይተናል፣
      የኑራም ይጣራል! ይጣራል! ይጣራል! ይጣራል!
የሰቆቃ ድምፆች ከሚነዱ ስልኮች ጎልፍ ያስተጋባል፣
      የሃኒያ የኢዝራም፣ ይጣራል! ይጣራል!
ስለደረጃዎች፣ ስለጥቀጥቀ ጭሱ፣ ማፊን ይናገራል፣
ዓይናቸው ቢፈስም፣ ስለህንፃው ቋያ አሁን ለመመስከር፣
በአካልም ቢለዩ፣ በውስጡ ከመኖር፣
      አንቶነም ይጣራል! ይጣራል! ይጣራል!
መልካም ሰላምታቸው፣ ከፊገግታቸው ጋ መንገድ ላይ ይመጣል፣
      አዋ! የማሪያም ይጣራል! ይጣራል! ይጣራል!
ከጭሱ ጋር አብሮ፣ የሁሉም ነፍሳቸው ወደላይ አርጓል
      ጮርቃው ጀረማያም! ይጣራል! ይጣራል!
መንደርተኛ ሆነ፣ ለመታት ኖረናል፣
ይኸው አሁን ደግሞ፣ ስለ አሟሟታቸው ዋቢ አድርገውኛል፣
ከሚነዱ ነፍሶች፣ የሚነዱ ድምፆች፣ ሁሌ ይሰሙኛል፣
ብዕሩ ስለሃቁ፣ ይመስክር ይሉኛል፣

45

Ligaya   calling
Mehdi   calling
we lived next door . . . what will you do for us?
the voices ask whenever I go out
or come back home   they want to know
why it burnt down in minutes like a matchbox
and where will I find justice and a home
for Nura's family of voices
Khadija's family of voices
for Malak's voice and Jessica's and Tuccu's
for Biruk and his mother's voice and Ali's voice and little Isaac
                calling   calling
calling   calling   calling   calling   calling

translated by
Chris Beckett
Wandsworth

የሊጋያ ድምፁዋ፤ ይጣራል! ይጣራል!
　　　ማህዲም ይጣራል! ይጣራል! ይጣራል!
ስለ ፖርብትናህ ምን አደረከ ይላል፤
ሁልዬም ስወጣ ድምፆች ይጮሃሉ፤
ዘወትር ስገባም ለማወቅ ይሻሉ፤
በክብሪት ሳጥን ውስጥ፤ ለምንድን ታጉረው እንደተቃጠሉ፤
የትነው መኖሪያ ቤት፤ ፍትህ ያለ ብለው ሁሌ ይጠይቃሉ፤
የኑራም ቤተሰብ፤ ድምፃቸው ይጮሃል፤
የከድጃም እናት፤ ድምፃቸው ይሰማል፤
የማላከም ድምፁ፤ የጀሲካ ድምፁዋ፤ ትኩም አበሮ ድምፁ
የብሩክ፤ የናቱ፤ የዓሊ፤ የይሳቅ ድምፅ፤ የዚያ የቀንበጡ
　　　　　ይጣራል! ይጣራል!
ይጣራል! ይጣራል! ይጣራል! ይጣራል! ይጣራል!

Alemu Tebeje
Lancaster West Estate
North Kensington

Witness

This is what's left:
pinned to a tree-trunk
messages to the dead,
calls to those who live.

Shrines lie by churches
and in doorways,
wilted flowers,
their price stickers peeled,
postcards and teddy bears,
virgins and buddhas
with their eyes lowered.

Everywhere are questions:
how, who, why?

From a hand-painted poster
hear the prophet lament:
Mine eye runneth down
with rivers of waters.
See how his tears stain
photos of the missing!

Bear witness
to what's on the wall:
The truth will not be hidden.

Caroline Maldonado
Acton

Safe Landing

The mum who dropped her baby from the tower
still haunts my dreams and every waking hour.
I've heard it said that when she threw you down
you landed safe below in arms unknown.

I cannot for your sake imagine this:
what pain before the binding farewell kiss?
What anguish as you hurtled through the air—
and did she see you landing safely there?

The upheld arms of one who gave his all
to save your fragile life after the fall
may well have been her cherished final sight
before she choked to death that ghastly night.

I hope, though, that she lived and found her way
out of the blaze into the wakening day
and that her baby in the shell-shocked queue
is held in her arms now. Let this be true.

The only comfort if she died is this:
she reasoned well before her good-bye kiss.
Better a single death (her own) than two;
no other life more dear to her than you.

I see her choking as the flames shoot high,
the black smoke rushing in. All round her lie
the charred remains of the un-numbered dead.
Is she among them? Nothing has been said.

The black tower looms against the London sky,
holding its secrets still as months go by.
Hers is one story. There are many more
who lost their lives that night for being poor.

Lucy Newlyn
Oxford

*

'This is not a poem, it is a letter . . .'

Marco and Gloria, this is not a poem, it is a letter
To those who sat next to me
On the direct plane to London
And asked me about how to settle there,
As someone who lived in England for 15 years
And then returned to her motherland.
So there I was, repeating the journey to Oxford,
but this time just for a short pleasure trip.

We talked, sitting next to each other
Consuming tea and British snacks.

> *'Where do we look for a home; how do we change money;*
> *What should we eat; what should we say or not say*
> *So as not to annoy the Brits?'*

After we went through passport control
I saw you guys going down the escalator
Holding hands. You turned
And gave me your smiles
Full of hope and life.

And now I see you in your online London photo album
With the air of residents rather than tourists.
One shot frames you against the background
Of a neoclassical British palace
Built in ivory stone with tall arches. Side by side
I see you in another holding two lagers:
Marco, in your Camden Market black leather jacket,
And you, Gloria, with shining freshly dyed hair.
The same open smiles, but now somewhat enigmatic.

'Questa non è una poesia, è una lettera . . .'

Marco e Gloria, questa non è una poesia, è una lettera
ai due italiani seduti accanto a me
sul volo diretto a Londra
che chiedevano come sistemarsi nella City,
ad una come me che aveva vissuto
in Inghilterra per 15 anni
ed era poi tornata alla sua madrepatria.
Quella volta stavo tornando ad Oxford
solo per un viaggio di piacere.

Chiacchierammo, seduti gomito a gomito,
consumando tè e snack britannici.

> *'Dove cercare casa, come cambiare gli euro?*
> *Cosa mangiare e non mangiare? Cosa dire e non dire*
> *per non infastidire gli inglesi?'*

Dopo il check-out dei passaporti, ragazzi, vi guardai
scendere con la scala mobile,
tenendovi per mano. Vi giraste
e mi donaste i vostri sorrisi
pieni di vita e speranza.

E vi guardo adesso nel vostro *photo-album*
su Facebook, a Londra, con l'aria di residenti, non turisti.
Uno scatto vi incornicia sullo sfondo
di un palazzo britannico in stile neoclassico,
costruito in pietra d'avorio, con alti archi. E, fianco a fianco,
vi vedo in un'altra foto mentre reggete due birre lager:
Marco, tu indossi una giacca di pelle nera stile Camden Market,
e tu, Gloria, hai capelli lucidi, da poco schiariti.
Gli stessi sorrisi aperti, ora, in qualche senso, enigmatici.

In two more pictures you are sitting
On a bench at Latimer Road tube station
And lying down on the grass in Hyde Park,
Recently employed, with an assured future in sight.

And I looked at you while I stared at the pillar of fire.
Gloria, you were texting your friend:
      'Remember me, I am dying.'
Marco, you were sitting on the floor,
face hidden in your hands.

It burned on, burned on, burned on, that fire,
And raised you to the sky for ever
Holding hands.

This is not a poem; it is a letter.
The poetry was in your smiles.

translation by the author

In altre due foto siete seduti
su una panchina alla stazione della metropolitana di Latimer Road
e poi sdraiati sull'erba, a Hyde Park,
da poco assunti, con un futuro assicurato davanti.

E vi guardo mentre fisso la pira di fuoco.
Gloria, tu mandi SMS alla tua migliore amica:
     'Ricordati di me, sto morendo.'
Marco, tu sei seduto sul pavimento, la faccia nascosta tra i palmi.

Continua ad ardere, ad ardere, ad ardere, quel fuoco,
E vi innalza verso il cielo per sempre
tenendovi per mano.

Questa non è una poesia; è una lettera.
La poesia è nei vostri sorrisi.

Erminia Passannanti
Salerno

On a Morning like This

On such a morning, when the sun promises relaxing heat,
and a friend is coming over to stay, the room is ready,
the menu planned, and thoughts of conversation and wine
keep me going through the last few tasks. When the garden
is nodding with flowers and greenery, and birds are busy,
when everything sparkles, and the beech leaves are silver
with light, coffee is brewing, breakfast celebrates waking up
on this new day.
It's hard to remember the people who won't see
another promising day, because lives have been stolen from them,
by bombs and fire, the uncaring world. When crowdfunding
comes too late for sprinkler systems and donations are locked away.
When they can no longer walk to shops to pick up milk, their clothes
moving in summer breeze, nor take exams, plan a future.
On a morning like this, it is hard to believe in such things.

Angela Topping
Northwich, Cheshire
*

The Chair

In London W11
a school.
In the school
a room.
In the room
a chair.
A chair that is empty.
A chair that waits.

But no one comes.
The chair is empty.

Here come words.
Words are flying.
The air is full of words,
and the words float down,
down on to the chair.
The chair
in the room.
The room
in the school.
The school
in London W11.

Michael Rosen
Haringey

Caoineadh

I summon to this
        shadow graveside
the joys and sorrows
        of our families.

My sister's wonder at sweet pea
blossoming on a cold windowsill.
The speckled palette of her view
across an unfamiliar London sky.

Her daughter's delight in dancing
in learning. Of *uaigneas*, loneliness
sadness, comforted by a letter
from home in her mother tongue.

Will anyone ask if she was happy?
If long hours cleaning hospital
wards bled her skin
        dampened her soul?

Does anyone care that she was good;
that she helped neighbours?
Her beliefs had no colour;
she is beloved, *grá geal mo chroí*.

That she missed music, singing
        her voice strong
a skylark in London
        keening for home?

Working to stay alive
    to flourish
        raise her family
           to be free.

Rona Fitzgerald
Glasgow

*

Status Update

I used to be window, now see only walls.
I listened for traffic, now hear only screams.
Things are not what they were.

I lived in a cell, now camp on the floor.
Once was high-riser, now blackened cracked tooth.
Things are not what they were.

I didn't stay put. I opened my door.
My landing had notice: no cyanide mentioned.
Things are not what they were.

I used to be stairwell, now am ground water.
I wanted confession, got wringing of hands.
Things are not what they were.

A used-to-be person, I'll now be memorial.
I was unheard but won't remain silent.
Things are just as they were.

Mark Cassidy
Havant

Schoolfriend

Sometimes you can't go back to sleep to
change a bad dream my Nan used to say
things like you can hide down a hole but . . . , wrap
up against the cold but . . . and never finish I used
to think it was nonsense then I saw her look at me and
wait for me to add the end so I'd say you can wrap

up against the	cold but you can't peel
off your skin if	it gets too hot and she'd
nod and she	said in rocky places
some flowers	find it hard to get a
hold others have	no trouble they are the

best because they surprise you with colour and just
being there but remembering all their names is hard
learning new words when there are hundreds is hard
I said to my Nan that morning I love the colour of

marmalade window glass	orange on the
side of the plate but a	window is not
a door and they needed a	door on the
way to school it was quiet	but there was
nothing quiet about that	lifeless baby

they pulled out nothing quiet at all I don't know how
they count with their arithmetic they can't never agree
I counted fewer in class today at break we listened to
voices singing and here and after tea I watched Nan
ironing you can fit more into a case or a drawer when
things are folded flat she said they fitted so many in
there I said to her I think they'd been ironed good and
proper she said they'll never really unpack that one.

M.T. Taylor
Glasgow

Potteric Carr, 15 June 2017

There's a catch
as the path leads through nature's reclamation
of the industrial wasteland,

a catch in the throat
that is soothed by the duck-down duvet
of these birds and trees,

a catch as the migraine
becomes a shadow of the siren
in the small hours,

a catch as the tension eases
and there's a purple heron out there, somewhere,
or just passing through,

a catch at the flash of metallic blue
which is a trailer on the skyline
travelling the M18,

a catch in the memory
triggered by the name of Grenfell,

a catch from Grenfell Tower
where the duck-down duvet is blue touchpaper,

a catch in the pictures seen on TV
where the building immolates as if doused in lighter fuel,

a catch in the throat from the acrid smoke and rain
of black flakes of fatal cladding,

a catch at the report
of a baby thrown to safety from a ninth floor window.

Richard Carpenter
York

Khadija Saye

I never knew her, or her work, until this day.

Her nascent fame had no time to flow
from Venetian waters to the galleries of the globe.

Curators' invitations remained unopened
while fast flames licked over her golden time,
her mother's hopes, her forefathers' dreams.

And no amount of water could bring them back,
though they tried, god knows, they tried.

I never knew her, but if I had passed her
on the streets of London, I would have met
her broad smile and the gleam of her bright eyes.

I never knew her, but I would have thanked her
for my introduction to places and people

I had never known. To the tall, turbaned tribesman,
to the sports hall splashed with bright prayer mats,
a pallet of robes and paired-up shoes,

to the girls in bikinis, and a feathered headdress,
black curves accented by a backdrop of snow,

to the barefooted child, to the sun on the sand,
to the man resting hands on his clapped-out VW,
boasting its badges to her lens.

I never knew her, but she showed me that
history can be written on the back of a head,

that neat plaits follow family lines,
tinted blonde sections defy conventions
and grand swirls crown her in all her glory.

I never knew her, but she gave me her eyes.

Adele Cordner
Magor, South Wales

*

The Twilight Shift

You glimpse our silhouettes
in green-tinted, vacated rooms
before you check-in your identity.
Will you avert your eyes?
Will you look through us?

Forgotten in the function room
behind a screen, when the party explodes,
our faces imprinted on glass.
If you slip into a smoky passageway
our uniform grey, our white sheets, will flash past.

Do you expect us to stay in this perpetual holding room?

Swapping curses in our endangered language?

When you fall back onto your bed
will you notice the clothes you didn't wear
rearranged in the wardrobe,
the furniture moved for silent dancing,
different flowers in the vase?
An otherly perfume
as if it is someone else's room.

David Keyworth
Scawby, North Lincolnshire

Grenfell Falls Through the Safety Net

The world is caught fast in a trap.
Earth, sea, air and water are poisoned so what.
Children scream and die clad in flames so what.
No escape only further ensnarement in poverty.
We can't stop hurricanes or bombs or council policy-
makers who mask bees' tracks, take the wild ones'
places, kill the people in their homes.

In the lane beside the ruined tower
sparrows dodge weeds zip past leaves
catch the low wind undercurrents of divine
matrix passageways to a nest, a berry, a seed of grass.
Lorries loaded with rubble rumble and bump
in their wake scattering the flock.

Nothing the poor can do their house is gone.
Even diamonds under intense mechanical pressure
shatter.
Even the soul gives way to an atomic wind.

Censorship is eliminating emotional reality
via mysterious technological wizardry.
Just pick any word like *unselfish* or *love* out of any hat.
All alike cloaked under the Emperor's radar.
His crowning glory is the way he tells it on the news.

Under the purr and murmur of the drones
passing over desert villages in the shadow
of the night the eye of the pyramid pulses in the desert.
Families flee looking for a place of safety.
The horizon is burning. They tread carefully every step a mile.

At the bottom of the pit of fascism
the lingua franca of business bubbles like magma.
Yet not a sparrow falls without God's holy care.
Our visions of ourselves are clouded from our sight
by constant blood.
Our sacred vision is fully absent sometimes.

A beautiful sunset casts light upon
what remains of Grenfell Tower.
People stream in bearing gifts
from the four corners of the city.
They are speaking the original language.
They are speaking in the tongue of angels.

Translation falters at the limits
of what the survivors can bear.
Their loved ones are in heaven
not trapped in a blasted world.

Sarah Connor
Trelights, Cornwall

Rapunzel

Moss Heights, Glasgow

Ur yi no feart? school pals wunner
Sae high up? Plump palms oan thi sill
she learns thi toon's clutter. Day-bricht
fitba pitches whare Daddy plays
unner floodlichts. Motors birl roon shinin
thi night. Barbie-pink curtains aye open.
Thi shoppin centre, whare thi wumman
upstairs works, jist a wee toy.
Hir magic show. Dancin wi thi wind,
thi swayin flats fuel hir dreams. Oer thi noise
o thi babby through thi wa greetin,
thi telly blethers
*A hundred people are now feared dead
in the Grenfell Tower's blaze.*
Streechin oot, freckles agin thi gless
she peers doon at hir buildin, wunners
Whit's cladding?

*Finola Scott
Glasgow*

Double Talk

Safety measures are firmly in place.
In the event of fire — 'Stay put'. We remain firmly in place.

We are looking into this problem.
Our windows crack, shatter. We are looking out of this problem.

These people need ironclad assurances.
We are clad in metal, polyethylene and foam. It is alight.

Steps are being taken to improve safety.
These steps are hotplates. They scald our feet as we run.

Here are the minutes of our last meeting.
Here are the minutes of our last hours.

Those responsible for the tragedy have been replaced.
Those affected by it can't be.

Our condolences rain down on you.
We had no sprinklers to do the same.

All efforts are being made to identify the causes.
Hope vanishes of you ever identifying our corpses.

Now we are ready to listen to your concerns.
Our lips are sealed. Our unheard voices are in your files.

John Lindley
Congleton, Cheshire

Aberfan & Grenfell

Like-a Coal Board an Council
they woz ignored by-a Tories
oo jest didn care.

Them yers o warnins,
the ewge tip movin;
cheap claddin, bare pipin.

Slurry o waste suffocatin
teachers, pupils, people in ouses,
lives changed ever an always.

Slike-a fire an smoke
so quick them flats a wick,
the outside wax drippin.

Screams choked by fumes
an black, thick sludge,
graves o rubble an tar.

Rescuers from ev'rywhere,
lines o elpers, each and
linked like valleys joinin.

Slowly we seen survivors
rise from devastation an ashes
t cry out — 'Yeah, we're still yer!'

Mike Jenkins
Merthyr Tydfil

Keeping Up Appearances

'The clue's in the name. Royal Borough.
We serve Knightsbridge, not Latimer Road.
We're here for our quality voters
With a moneyed and tasteful postcode.
We tolerate you since we have to
And we hope that you'll soon move elsewhere.
Until then we'll do our legal duty.
If you cause any problems—beware!

Your flats are all crumbling eyesores.
Your neighbours are your social betters.
They paid millions to live in this area—
Some are next door to scroungers and debtors.
So it's time to refurbish your building.
Not with fire doors, sprinklers and care
But with cladding to make it look nicer
So the rich can pretend you're not there.

It's unsafe, you complain. That's just rubbish.
We've been running it that way for years.
Just be grateful you're housed in this borough
And make sure that you're not in arrears!
You've new skins on your homes. They look lovely.
Regulations and standards are met.
All done legally and within budget
So get on with your lives and don't fret.'

Those new skins caused a ghastly inferno.
But that council is still in control
Though some should be charged with manslaughter
And the rest all relieved of their role.
Now the people cry 'Justice for Grenfell!'
In the name of those folk left alone
In a world where appearances mattered
More than flesh, skin, hair, muscle and bone.

Attila the Stockbroker
Southwick, West Sussex

Fred Engels in the Gallery Café

does it feel odd to you
the old man lights his pipe
rooms where you sat are now
thin air is anyone sitting here
no no take it   the stench
of pipe tobacco   *when one individual*
inflicts upon another   he's wearing a
handsome frock coat   No Smoking Allowed
such injury that death   I'm sorry
I'll be back shortly   *results we*
call the deed   more heart-rending
tales of separation   *manslaughter*   there is
shall we say a burning anger
in this room   *when the assailant*
before thought how do we measure
malice   our so-called comfort runs
to   *knew in advance*   the exit
strategy   Stay In Your Homes   *that*
the injury would be fatal   on
the eighteenth floor   *we call his*
deed murder   all the latest breaking
hearts   *but when society*   is this
chair free coffee with a hint
of almonds   *deprives thousands of the*
necessaries of life   today's specials board
the stairwells filled with black smoke
forces them to remain in such
conditions   milk chocolate and blueberry notes
that death occurs   this place is
where the middle class conduct affairs

in the novel I just read
and permits these conditions to remain
we sailed from Dubrovnik to Split
lovely pictures   *that deed is murder*
not wanting to be trapped his
square hipster beard dropping their kids
from bedroom windows *as surely as that*
coffee's cheap but the cake's rich
in this place   *of the single*
individual   whose theory of surplus value
squeezes another cup from the teapot

Steven Waling
Manchester
*

Pity the Woman Made of Wood

Crowned temporary Empress
of this tragic bit of chipboard floating
off the northernmost coast
of what used to be Europe.

Open please your hearts, empty your heads
and pretend not to notice the predictable few
disfigured old bastards who operate her,
yanking the all too visible wires
that make her jaws clack
awkwardly up and down. Pity please
this woman made of wood
now she's too well understood
and gets all the kicks and expletives,
when she tries to speak about
anything other than the quarterly accounts.

Her back burdened and bent.
Respect please the enormity
of the pearls she must bear
about her splintering neck.
And don't be behind with the rent
or petition her to save you when you again
characteristically fail to save yourself.

When smoke curls black under your door
you can snore on unperturbed in your narrow little bed,
bought with a pay-day loan obtained—quite legally—
from a bloke reputed to give defaulters
cement flip-flops for Christmas, to take them safely
down one of the larger pipes that joyfully
pour shit into the River Styx.

But the woman made of wood,
must at all costs avoid
unguarded flames for she would go up
like a cheap deckchair that picked the wrong
day to go sunbathing at Hiroshima.

Think of this, please, when bawling
your lucky human screams
as the fire arrives quite matter-of-fact
to oxidize you to a small hill of ashes
around what looks like
a collar bone. No such luck
for the woman made of wood.

Kevin Higgins
Galway
*

Bring it Home

Bring help
Bring fire engines
Bring water
Bring air
Bring stretchers
Bring ambulances
Bring us round from sleep and out to safety

Bring food
Bring clothes
Bring blankets
Bring camp beds
Bring phone chargers so we can find our friends and family
And tell them that we made it

Bring shoulders to cry on
Bring arms to embrace
Bring ears to listen
Bring hands to hold
Bring the strength to go on

Bring news
Bring hope
Bring solidarity
Bring community
Bring what you can
Bring yourself

Bring questions
Demand answers
Bring the letters written and the warnings given
And bring the inadequate replies

Bring the plans
Bring the regulations
Bring the budgets
Bring the decisions and the contracts
Let everyone examine them

Bring your despair, your pain
And blend it in solidarity with others'
Bring it to the boil
Bring it into the enquiry room
And into the corridors of power
Bring the truth out into the open
Bring justice
Bring charges
Bring this system down

Janine Booth
Hackney
*

The Ballad of John Grenfell

John Grenfell was a captain bold.
The Chilean flag he flew,
and fought her wars at Cochrane's side.
Brazil employed them too.

Lost his right arm on *Caboclo*
before Buenos Aires, under Norton;
married Dolores at Montevideo;
then hoisted his flag in '41.

Brazilian consul, Liverpool,
he held *Alfonso*'s trial
with family and nobby guests—
a pleasure trip in style.

But *Ocean Monarch* sailed that day.
A migrant ship was she,
with exiles fleeing Ireland's blight
for lands across the sea.

When flames roared out, in sight of land,
winds hurled them through the ship
and drove the wretches overboard
like beasts before a whip.

Alfonso closed to two ships' length
and lowered launches—four.
The crippled Admiral led one;
a Marquis took an oar.

Two hundred souls were saved that day;
Alfonso took off most.
But near that number drowned away,
with many children lost.

The Admiral's guests stripped off their clothes
and gave to those in need.
Brazil's Infanta? Duchesse d'Aumale? —
they paid their rank no heed.

Not everything was worse back then.
Those privileged feared God,
acknowledged fellow citizens,
and minded duty's code.

The laws were harsh, near pitiless;
and charity was scarce.
The noose or convict chains for those
who touched what wasn't theirs.

But woe betide the public man
who preyed upon the poor,
who scanted by-laws, looked for bribes,
or fudged official chores.

They buried John in Père Lachaise,
where other heroes lie.
If he could see these latter days
he'd let some sea oaths fly!

Rip Bulkeley
Oxford
*

Minimizing Disruption

Ladbroke Grove used to have a Dub Vendor store
At number 150. Now that shop sells mobile phones.
I can remember some of the vinyl I bought from there.
A Delroy Wilson album with 'Better Must Come'.
Michael Prophet's 'Gunman'
Wayne Smith, Tenor Saw
('Victory Train' on a twelve alongside all his big tunes on pre)
All the Jammys and Taxi and George Phang tunes
That soundtracked my twenties.

And 'Murderer'.
Murderer by Buju Banton.
Murderer by Barrington Levy.
The Buju tune goes 'Murderer blood is on your shoulders
Kill I today you cannot kill I tomorrow'.

There are 'Missing' posters plastered all round Ladbroke Grove.
The faces of the missing who are the not-yet-officially-dead
Of Grenfell Tower, which stands now
A 24-storey fire-black column
Sucking all the light out of this year's spring
And shadowing the Grove.
Not far from here Aswad recorded 'Live and Direct',
Meanwhile Gardens, Carnival, 1983.
Music made to make you feel like a warrior;
Bassline thunder and Brinsley Forde yelling 'Murderah',
And the crowd all ravin' and shoutin' 'Murderah'.
But no-one's ravin' now.

Mothers throwing babies from windows.
'The £10m building refurbishment, which included
the installation of insulated exterior cladding,
was a complex one as it took place
with all 120 flats occupied throughout. The logistics
had to be carefully managed to minimize disruption.'
Mothers throwing babies from windows;
The windows all blown out now.
You can still see shreds of curtains
And the patterns on some—a horse, an owl
Cauterized, flapping.

At the next meeting of the full council at K&C
Shout 'Murderah, murderah'
Till all of them reach jail
Let us be the raging brothers and sisters of the burned-alive
Shouting endlessly 'murderah, murderah, murderah'.

Another tune I remember buying at **Dub Vendor**
Johnny Osbourne 'Thirteen Dead, Nothing Said',
And the Linton Kwesi Johnson album
'Making History'
With the track 'New Cross Massakeh'.
John La Rose called the New Cross fire
'an unparalleled act of barbaric violence
against the black community'.

I guess history teaches us to be wary
Of words like 'unparalleled'.

Nick Moss
Brent
*

77

we walk in silence

we sign the petition that comes around that is going off to the Prime Minister raging against the years of neglect that led to Grenfell

we sign the petition online raging against the closure of Ladbroke Grove library so that a private prep-school can take its place

we read that the councilor who made that decision already had his 3-year-old child enrolled in that school

but we walk in silence

we take walks in our lunch-hours around the area and see the skyline littered with cranes that at night look like the red eyes of a sky-monster

the same cranes that are rebuilding this area, after it has been pulled down and evacuated, with chrome and glass balconies that have million-pound price tags attached to each flat

but we walk in silence

we live in flats all of our lives; flats that our mothers and grandmothers lived in on tenancies that they owned but which now will be passed on to our children for a period of five years before they get reviewed out of them and moved onto the streets

but we walk in silence

we see our old youth clubs being knocked down, our libraries shut, our playgrounds shut, the same playgrounds we played kiss-chase in and smoked our first cigarette in, drunk our first can of beer in, playgrounds our children cannot play in any more because there are construction workers in them turning them all into more blocks of luxury flats

but we walk in silence
not because we aren't angry
not because we aren't raging
but because we hope that everyone else will understand
that it is because we have no voice
any more

Martin Hayes
Westminster

The Search

Circling days while ash falls,
another white face offers condolences,
you shake your head and want to stab them.

The traffic roars and pavements crack.
From habit, you reach out to lean on an arm
that isn't there.

Scorched litter memories scatter and whirl,
the voice of a child never sleeps.
You excuse yourself, mind blurring, befuddled,

and barter with God, scrape the earth with
raw fingernails, a red-eyed animal howling.
They step back, and give you a contact number.

Beda Higgins
Newcastle upon Tyne

Finger Pointing

The finger says: I am so dark against the sky
because I am here to teach you about aftermaths,
that bleak sense of waste on the tongue,
the drip of rain through ruined rooms
picked over by pigeons, by the raw air.
I am the reminder of terrors
that warp the mind, mountains too high
for anyone to place one foot upon
without turning away, wrecked and inconsolable.
My darkness means it will take you years
to notice behind me there are clouds,
sometimes sun, that the sky will change subtly,
like waves washing in and creeping out.
Who will even notice that thunder falls
less often, that the silences are longer?
Perhaps the homeless man in the street,
the family living in one room, the migrant, the couple
holding hands in the hope
there can be a future.

Norton Hodges
Lincoln
*

Another View of the City

'Along here,' you're saying, 'please.
These are some of their finest houses.'

Incoming summer clouds threaten
to sluice this richest of boroughs.

And we're not so far now from where
the demarcation lines blur

between photogenic mews,
wide streets that would be avenues

and the instant democracies
of franchise cafés and the Tube.

Gated, these places you'd have us take
as aspiration made good on your terms

look a lot like an exclusion zone —
with us here as inadvertent tourists

caught on surveillance cameras.
They've invested in themselves

behind these black iron fences
with credit that's hardly creditable.

You're too good to see it yourself
or the absence of welcome

in a lone dog-walker's eye
while even now you extol

manifestations of their success
as if there were no victims.

And if there were no victims,
accumulations of wealth and debt

might not leave us seeing red
as the sky we're watching deepens

and tower-block shadows advance
like promises, like omens.

Tom Phillips
Sofia

눈물 자국

하연 임 선화

눈물 마른 자국일까
새싹 하나 돋는다

세찬 태풍 지난후
침묵만이 남은곳

남 몰래
돋아난 연한 새싹
햇빛 찾아 고개든다.

Rivulets

Through dried tear ducts spring unripe rivulets of green,
Silence drifts through the land
Toughened by the violence of the storm.
Peacefully, quietly, infant buds seek the warmth of the sun.

Sun Hwa Griffiths
Framfield, East Sussex
translation by the author
*

The Throw

my son brought me from Thailand is magenta,
a royal marriage of violet and pink.
When I lay it on my bed over the quilt
from India it becomes an extra skin,
one that's kind to my uncomfortable body.

How I love its minute gold elephants, each
the size of the top segment of my little finger.
They walk in perfect lines, head to tail,
along the embroidered roads of the fabric
and when I stroke one an elephant god appears,

becomes the memory of riding in a high place
on a huge blur of animal, becomes the elephants
living in Mimi's flat. My son has elaborated
on the heat in Thailand but here winter is trying
to sneak into the house and steal its warmth.

I creep into bed, invite the elephants to tiptoe
across my body's pathways. When snowflakes
begin to float whitely down I close my eyes
and they melt into the soft purplish mystery
of nothing where I wish pain, all pain to vanish.

Myra Schneider
Enfield
*

85

the morning afterwards

still rubbing sleep
from nightweary eyes
when i saw it
the morning
afterwards
blackened eyes
in a face of grief
staring out at me
from the charred stones
through white smoke
high up on the right
a pigeon flew
with its beak open
i heard
its cry
searching, like me
for its nest
for its home
in vain

translation by
Rip Bulkeley

am morgen danach

rieb noch den schlaf
von nachtmüden lidern
als ich es sah
am morgen
danach
augen geschwärzt
trauerumrandet
starrten mich an
aus verbranntem gestein
durch weissen rauch
hoch oben rechts
flog eine taube
den schnabel geöffnet
ich hörte
den schrei
sie suchte wie ich
das nest
das heim
umsonst

Elisabeth Sofia Schlief
Bonn

The Role of Bluest Reason

The climate engineers
pull the world in that direction
with important dark green impulses.

They are all guests of fall
and sleep in white hotels
in a silence hung with bells.

Clouds have slowed down, unable
to tolerate the pain; winds become
too weak to pass the winter in joy.

Won't the earth finally become conscious
of that heavy gasping, wind-aided spread
of buoyant hot gas under the ceiling?

Floor furnace, unprotected steel members,
the door swells into a foam, spray-on
protection flames into droplets

on plastic hinges and poured concrete.
Simply as a heat sink, aluminium cladding
stresses into the cooler wood, a maze of fine cracks

and air voids. The whole building behaves
like a semi-rigid Vulcan
due to access concerns, like painted-on snow.

I used to be self-righteous,
lots of church in me, till rain
weakened the leaves like the final stages

in the preparation of silk. But yes,
I'm more and more from this place,
its aesthetics of repair.

The moon made male patterns
in the lookbook, the patterned moon
split the clouds to a water war,

then a cross of lilies and fern.
The stars were playing themselves
on their first journey to the sun

till dawn came hurtling through
the curtains, unwrapping the envelope
of the footprint intact on the windless moon.

Medbh McGuckian
Belfast

From a Sheet of Paper

This is the letter to the Tower
that I cannot write.
It rains on me in flakes of char.
When I wake, I see a fire that weeps
and a glow of eyes that grows enormous.
Out of wound, the want.
What to build? And how?
Through my window, an early sun
rising over London.

Joan Michelson
Haringey

Conflagration

Conflagration is a word it is a con it is a flag it is not rationed out once it begins it is generous this is what that one deserves that one needs that one will have.

Some seeds you do not understand they are pebbles under your feet you do not recognize them as seeds.

Fire changes things it runs up a flag it limns the seams with flame it unpicks stitches it is not a con it uses everything up it makes things other you need to breathe. You are thinking it is exhausting when your ration of oxygen is exhausted you will die.

The streets are full of flags a flag is a scrap of cloth flags flap at windows flags flutter down like rags and that's your ration up in smoke they make things other.

And there are seeds you do not understand. The seeds that lie like stones in the earth fire burns they have their ration of heat and crack open wide like glass like plastic and when fire is exhausted when all there is are blackened stumps and ash they split and burst open. You are thinking it exhausts you. You think that all that's left after fire is ash and cinders and gutters thick with a ration of death and flagstones dank with grease a thin plume of smoke still running up the bills.

There are ideas you do not recognize you think they are a con. We want clean streets we want our flag to mean something our flag is exhausted it makes things other we think it is a con.

The seeds are not a con the fire cannot kill them the oxygen being exhausted cannot kill them. You can be rational you can take the seeds you do not recognize you can let them grow. This is the dream of the seeds. What is the exhaustion of a fire but a lack of oxygen? You can still breathe. There are seeds you would not recognize they whirl in the heat they fly miles to land who knows where some seeds you do not recognize as seeds until there is a fire.

Lindy Newns
Manchester

The Heroes on the Stair

Look for the sun to rise again
From the darkness of your heart
In this hour of sorrow
We must stand by each other
Not drift apart
The dawn will surely come to us
If the night be red with fear
For the shadows at the window
And the heroes on the stair
Yes, the dawn will surely come to us
If the night be red with fear
For the shadows at the window
And the heroes on the stair

Look for the truth beyond the lies
Look for the dawn to come
Look for a road that leads to hope
For all, not just for some
The truth will surely come to us
Our journey will not cease
Not till we have justice
Not till we have peace
If there is no justice
How can there be peace?
If there is no justice . . .

André Rostant
Newham
*

Notes and Acknowledgements

7   **Grenfell, 2018** was published on the *London Grip* and *Culture Matters* websites in February 2018.

10   **High-Rise** was previously published in the *Morning Star*, 6 July 2017: www.morningstaronline.co.uk/a-7e3e-Al-Mcclimens-High-rise#.Wf-swBE27LL8

11   **Border Patrol** was first published in Matt Barnard, *Anatomy of a Whale*, The Onslaught Press, 2018.

12   **The Bunker** An earlier version appeared in the music fanzine *Belly Dance* in May 1995.

14   **A Report from the Border** appeared in Anne Stevenson, *A Report from the Border*, Bloodaxe, 2003.

15   **Wrong Move** Despite adding that the flat was no longer available, two property websites were still carrying this advertisement in February 2018, in one case complete with photographs.

16   **Post Mortem** The Great Fire of Rome began in the late evening of 18 July 64 CE. It raged for six days. Tacitus wrote his account of it in 116 CE.

18   **Partitions, 1982** The epigraph comes from: William Wordsworth, *The Prelude*, Book VIII, 823–30. An earlier version of this poem appeared in Steve Griffiths, *Selected Poems*, Seren Books, 1993.

22   **Red Watch** is based on the author's experience as head of Maxilla Nursery School from 2008 to 2015. The school was five minutes walk from Grenfell Tower.

24   **Field of Crimson** The Great Fire of London destroyed the homes of about 87% of the city's inhabitants over four days in early September 1666. Historians disagree about the likely number of fatalities.

25   **And in the Air Death Moans and Sings** revisits 'Into Battle', a famous British poem of the First World War by Julian Henry Francis Grenfell.

26   **The Firefighter** was read by an actor on BBC Radio 5 Live on 17 September 2017: http://www.bbc.co.uk/news/av/uk-41298320/grenfell-tower-a-fireman-s-memories-in-poetry

The Death of Children first appeared in Richard Berengarten, *The* 30
Blue Butterfly, Salt Publishing, Cambridge, 2007.

Hanako Paints Hiroshima appeared in the *Kent & Sussex Poetry Society* 34
Folio in 2016.

this grief is partisan was published in *New Verse News* on 19 June 2017: 36
https://newversenews.blogspot.co.uk/2017/06/this-grief-is-partisan.html

Carnival The Notting Hill Carnival is celebrated in late August on the 37
streets of the London borough which included Grenfell Tower. In
2017, just two months after the fire, revellers at the 51st Carnival held
a minute's silence on both days of the event.

In this Space We do Not Breathe The photographic artist Khadija 38
Saye (1992–2017) died alongside her mother Mary Mendy in Grenfell
Tower on 14 June 2017. Ms Saye's group of self-portraits, 'Dwellings:
in this Space we Breathe', was exhibited in Britain's Diaspora Pavilion
at the 2017 Venice Biennale. After the fire a BBC documentary about
that achievement by Ms Saye and her fellow exhibitors, scheduled for
17 June, was postponed until 2 September.

Safe Landing Few poets are investigative journalists, historians, or 49
lawyers. For at least two months after the fire, while most of these
poems were being written, some press reports included statements that
now appear inaccurate, and other versions of events may also be
disproved by further investigation. Poetry, however, is restricted to the
perceived event, as compared with more accurate accounts that may
come with hindsight. The poem thus reflects the feelings of millions
of people at the time.

On a Morning like This An earlier version appeared in *International* 54
Times on 27 June 2017.

Caoineadh means 'lament' or 'elegy' in Irish Gaelic. 56

Khadija Saye See previous note on Ms Saye. 60

Rapunzel The heroine in the Grimm Brothers' fairy-tale is a teenager 64
imprisoned at the top of an enchanted tower.

66 **Aberfan & Grenfell** On 21 October 1966 a colliery spoil tip slid down the mountain above the village of Aberfan in South Wales, engulfing the nursery school and taking the lives of 116 children and 28 adults. An official enquiry into the disaster laid the blame for it on the National Coal Board.

68 **Fred Engels in the Gallery Café** Phrases in italics are from: Frederick Engels, *The Condition of the Working Class in England in 1844*, John W. Lovell, New York, 1887, 63–4.

70 **Pity the Woman Made of Wood** was first published on *The Pileus* website on 27 June 2017: www.thepileus.com/culture/pity-the-woman-made-of-wood/

72 **Bring it Home** was first published on www.janinebooth.com on 14 June 2017, and then in *Solidarity 443* on 30 June 2017.

74 **The Ballad of John Grenfell** Eyewitness accounts confirm that the dignitaries undressed as far as Victorian decency allowed.

During the age of sail, Thomas Cochrane was perhaps the most formidable fighting seaman to reach the rank of Admiral in the Royal Navy. His exploits have been retold by several novelists, including C.S. Forester and Patrick O'Brian.

The Père Lachaise cemetery in Paris holds the remains of many famous people — Molière, Balzac, Chopin, Oscar Wilde, Edith Piaf, Jim Morrison, François Truffaut, and so on. To some of us, it is better known as the place where the surviving leaders of the Paris Commune were executed by firing squad on 28 May 1871.

Sources for Grenfell's life and this true story include the *Allgemeine Zeitung* (Munich), 7 December 1826; *O Spectador Brasileiro*, 1826, no. VIII; *Liverpool Mercury*, 25 August 1848; the Grenfell family history website: http://www.grenfellhistory.co.uk/; and the Brazilian Navy's historical website: http://www.naval.com.br/ngb/M/M018/M018-1CO.htm

76 **Minimizing Disruption** An earlier version, 'The exact reverse is true', was published at proletarianpoetry.com on 27 September 2017.

81 **Finger Pointing** is forthcoming in Norton Hodges, *Bare Bones*, The High Window Press, Grimsby, 2018.

84 **눈물 자국** was published in *The Sijo Life*, Sijo Saing' Hwal Publishers, 2017

The Throw was published in Myra Schneider, *The Door to Colour*, 85
Enitharmon Press, 2014.

The Heroes on the Stair The song from which these lyrics are taken 92
can be heard here: www.facebook.com/andre.rostant.5/videos/
vb.1743798897/ 10203455847953891/?type=2&theater

About the Poets

Alemu Tebeje is an Ethiopian exile poet who lost several neighbours in the fire. His poems have appeared in various magazines and anthologies. His play *Tamrat in the Cyclops' Cave*, written with Chris Beckett, was broadcast on BBC Radio 4 on 18 April 2017.

Attila the Stockbroker has earned his living as a poet since 1981, doing more than 3500 gigs in 24 countries. He writes poetry for people who don't like poetry.

Matt Barnard's debut collection *Anatomy of a Whale* was published in 2018 by The Onslaught Press. He was born in London, where he still lives with his wife and two sons.

Christine Barton was formerly the Head of Maxilla Nursery School and Children's Centre, then located close to Grenfell Tower. Children and families who had attended the Centre died in the fire.

Meg Barton used to work as a project manager. Her poems have appeared in a few magazines and anthologies and she has read at local poetry events.

Chris Beckett grew up in Ethiopia in the days of Haile Selassie. He loves Ethiopian culture, especially the poetry, music and food. Luckily, these can be found around London as well as in Ethiopia itself!

Richard Berengarten was born in London in 1943. He has lived in Greece, Italy, the USA and former Yugoslavia. His books include *The Manager*, *The Blue Butterfly*, *Notness*, *Manual*, and *Changing* (Shearsman).

Margaret Beston is a linguist, surprised by poetry in recent years! She is the founder of Roundel, a Poetry Society Stanza based in Tonbridge: www.roundelpoetrytonbridge.com

Janine Booth writes rebellious poetry and performs it at gigs, readings, festivals, protests and other events in Britain and abroad. She is a socialist, feminist, trade unionist and railway worker.

Rip Bulkeley is an award-winning Antarctic historian and the founder, in 1999, of Oxford's thriving Back Room Poets. His collection *War Times* was published by Ripostes in 2003.

Rachel Burns is currently an Arvon/Jerwood mentee in playwriting. While a young mum, she lived in social housing in a deprived area. She volunteers with a prisoners' charity providing support in court to defendants and their families.

Richard Carpenter is a retired General Practitioner and always considered his profession a privilege. He now has time to explore the world, and power, of poetry.

Mark Cassidy writes in the gaps between radiography and bird-watching, with the company of two rabbits, seven trees and his family. He looks at the world as it is.

Sharon D. Cohagan writes short fiction and poetry. She runs a creative writing class in Bonn, and is currently working on a volume of bilingual poetry.

Sarah Connor is a writer who lives in Cornwall and works as a carer in the community.

When **Adele Cordner** is not looking after her four children, three dogs and two cats, she enjoys writing and performing.

Andrew Dixon grew up on the Wirral. He is a scientist by profession.

S.O. Fasrus is a social justice activist and social research interviewer. Besides publishing articles in national newspapers and magazines, she writes serious poems and comic verse on politics and current affairs.

Rona Fitzgerald worked on promoting gender equality for twenty years at European and national levels. She writes poems about people and about matters in the world that concern her.

John Greening's most recent collection is *To the War Poets*, Carcanet, 2013. His memoir of life in Upper Egypt, *Threading a Dream*, has just appeared, and Eyewear will publish his collected essays in 2018: www.johngreening.co.uk

Steve Griffiths has published seven books of poems, most recently *Late Love Poems*, Cinnamon Press, 2016. He was a community and welfare rights worker, and a researcher into inequality.

Sun Hwa Griffiths writes Korean Traditional Poetry and leads a group of other poets working in that form. She also teaches poetry, song, and dance for senior citizens.

Martin Hayes has worked for 25 years in Kensal Road, off Ladbroke Grove. Some of the people he works with or previously worked with over the years lost relatives and life-long friends in the Grenfell tragedy.

Beda Higgins has published two collections of short stories, also poems in various anthologies. She has three grown-up children and a grandson, and when not writing, works as a Nurse in General Practice.

Kevin Higgins's *Song of Songs 2.0: new & selected poems* was published in 2017 by Salmon. The Stinging Fly magazine has described Kevin as 'likely the most read living poet in Ireland'.

Norton Hodges is a widely published poet and translator. *Bare Bones*, poems selected from twenty years writing, is published by The High Window Press, 2018.

Mike Jenkins writes fiction as well as poetry. He co-edited *Red Poets* magazine for over 23 years, and blogs on www.mikejenkins.net. His latest books are *Sofa Surfin*, Carreg Gwalch, and *Bring the Rising Home!,* Culture Matters, with paintings by Gustavius Payne.

Peter A. Kelly sometimes draws or photographs but usually writes instead. He has won one poetry prize, but is best rewarded by the effect on others of the completed work.

David Keyworth was born in West Bromwich but grew up in North Lincolnshire. In 2013 he won a new poet's bursary in the Northern Writing Awards. His first published poem was on a beer mat.

Gillian Laker was Poet of the Year for the Canterbury Festival in 2013 and also writes fiction. She is currently taking an MA in Creative Writing at the University of Kent.

Helen Laycock writes poetry, short stories, flash fiction and playlets. She has written several books for children.

Emma Lee blogs at http://emmalee1.wordpress.com. Her latest collection is *Ghosts in the Desert*, IDP, 2015, and she co-edited *Over Land, Over Sea: poems for those seeking refuge*, Five Leaves, 2015.

John Lindley is a freelance poet, songwriter and creative writing tutor. He runs workshops for writers' groups and festivals, in prisons, schools, universities, and day care centres, and for those with learning difficulties.

Julie Lumsden was an army child so grew up in many places. She lives with her husband, and their son lives and works in Sheffield city centre. Shoestring published her latest poetry collection.

Bernadette Lynch lives between England and Ireland, and writes about what is between and beyond. She is a member of reading and writing groups in County Roscommon, Maryland USA, and Birmingham, Clun and Newent.

Al McClimens is a soon-to-be-unemployed graduate of Sheffield Hallam University's M.A. Writing programme. He listens to Radio 3. These two facts are not thought to be connected.

Tom McColl writes poetry, flash fiction and short stories. He used to work as a bookseller, and now works at the Vote Office in the House of Commons.

Medbh McGuckian has published twenty collections. Her work was celebrated and explored in *The Poetry of Medbh McGuckian*, Cork University Press, 2010.

Caroline Maldonado is a poet and translator, published by Indigo Dreams and Smokestack Books. She worked for many years with migrants and refugees.

Joan Michelson was born in the USA but has lived in Britain for many years. Her new collection *Landing Stage*, SPM Publishers, 2017, concerns the lives of refugees and immigrants, including Syrians, Bosnians, and survivors of the Second World War.

Nick Moss grew up in Liverpool but now lives in London. He has been writing poetry since his release from prison two years ago. His work has appeared in *Magma, Proletarian Poetry, & New River Press Yearbook*.

Lucy Newlyn is a retired Oxford professor and the author of two collections of poetry. Her memoir *Diary of a Bipolar Explorer* will be published by Signal Books in 2018.

Lindy Newns lives in Manchester. In her third age, she wants to seed and spread words which will work for social justice. 'That which does not kill us makes us stronger.'

Ricky Nuttall is a London firefighter who attended the Grenfell Tower fire that fateful night. He has been writing poetry since adolescence as a coping mechanism for life and an expression of self.

Erminia Passannanti is an Italian writer and former member of Back Room Poets in Oxford. After living and teaching there for fifteen years she is now back in her motherland.

Tom Phillips is a poet, playwright and translator whose publications include *Recreation Ground*, Two Rivers Press, 2012, and *Unknown Translations*, Scalino, 2016. He also edits the magazine *Balkan Poetry Today*.

Sam Phipps grew up in Notting Hill. He writes poems and journalism.

Neil Reeder works as a researcher on public services. Poetry has been a mainstay of self-expression for him since his twenties, and his poems have been published in various magazines.

Michael Rosen has been writing poems for 55 years.

André Rostant is a single father with Trinidadian and Irish parents. He is a member of the Association of Calypsonians (UK) and plays with the Nostalgia Steelband. Their panyard is Maxilla Social Club, in the shadow of Grenfell.

Abigail Elizabeth Rowland writes poetry and short fiction from her home in Penzance in Cornwall. She is a lifelong socialist.

Elisabeth Sofia Schlief has been writing since early youth. She participates in writing groups, readings, anthologies and broadcasts, and is currently working on her second collection.

Myra Schneider has published several collections of poetry, mainly with Enitharmon Press. Other publications include books about personal writing. She is a poetry tutor and believes in the power of poetry.

Finola Scott likes writing and tickling her grandchildren. A Slam-winning granny, she appeared this year at the EIBF as well as reading in Rosslyn Chapel by candlelight.

Jane Spiro joins up poetry, the violin and teaching international students. She has published a novel (Crucible Press 2001), two poetry collections (Oversteps), and stories for language learners. She writes as a leap into other lives.

Anne Stevenson has published sixteen collections and numerous other books on poets and poetry, of which the most recent is *About Poems and how Poems are not About*, Bloodaxe, 2017. Her influence and example run deep and clear through much of British poetry today.

Chelsea Stockham is fairly new to poetry, despite writing for almost her entire life. Along with film, she considers it one of her favourite art forms.

George Szirtes is a Hungarian-born poet and translator, author of many books, and winner of the TS Eliot Prize 2004.

M.T. Taylor writes from a high spot from where she can see for miles, even in rain. She tries to keep a sense of perspective and an eye on things.

Angela Topping is the author of eight collections of poetry, four pamphlets and three critical books: angelatopping.wordpress.com/ She is a former writer in residence at Gladstone's Library.

Steven Waling has published several books, including *Travelator*, Salt, 2007, and has many poems in magazines and online.

Pat Winslow's most recent collection is *Kissing Bones*, Templar Poetry, 2012. For more information, see www.patwinslow.com and https://thepatwinslow.blogspot.co.uk/

Lightning Source UK Ltd.
Milton Keynes UK
UKHW01f1826270518
323283UK00001B/46/P